Who's that fearsome
fish cruising just
beneath the surface?

Blue shark

WHO, ME?

It's a shark, one of the world's oldest and fiercest fish.

Great white shark

Who you calling OLD?

Sharks have some serious skills.

Spinner sharks can leap five feet (1.5 m) in the air!

Great white sharks have a bite four times as strong as a lion's!

Mako sharks can zip through the water at 60 miles an hour (97 km/h)!

Let's face it:

Sharks are...

SO
COOL!

Great white shark

Ooh...
YEAH!

Sharks live in every ocean. Bull sharks can even swim in freshwater rivers!

FINS FAR AND WIDE

BLUE SHARKS are common. And they sure do get around! They cruise in deep waters off every continent except Antarctica.

GREENLAND SHARKS are in no rush. They swim sluggishly in the frigid Arctic Ocean and live longer than any other shark—sometimes more than **400** years!

10

Da na. Da na. Da na ... Just kidding!

Bull shark

SILKY SHARKS like warm water. Scientists even spotted these sharks, along with hammerheads, living in an underwater volcano!

GOBLIN SHARKS don't fear the dark. Lurking in the lightless depths, they've been called living fossils because they've changed so little since prehistoric times.

Sharks have been around for **400** million years, since before the dinosaurs.

Fossilized megalodon tooth

SHARKOSAURUS

Imagine bumping into a prehistoric predator that could swallow a small boat! As large as a submarine, the mighty megalodon was a supersize version of the great white. It preyed on dinosaurs and prowled the seas as recently as 1.5 million years ago before going extinct. Fossils of its one-foot (30-cm)-long teeth have washed up on beaches around the world.

DINOSAURS?
Sounds
scary.

Shortfin mako shark

13

There are more than **500** species of sharks. They come in all shapes...

Something FUNNY about my shape?

Hammerhead shark

... and sizes!

EXTREME SHARKS

Whale sharks, like the one to the left, are the world's biggest fish, growing as large as a school bus! Let's dive deep and look at some other spectacular species ...

Basking shark

BASKING SHARKS use their mega mouths to scoop small creatures from the water.

Saw shark

SAW SHARKS swing their toothy snouts to stun fish.

PYGMY SHARKS are among the teeniest sharks.

Pygmy shark

Swell shark

SWELL SHARKS bend in a V-shape and swallow seawater to swell up to twice their normal size!

FRILLED SHARKS look like eels, but they're definitely sharks!

Frilled shark

Sharks don't worry about losing their sharp teeth—they have thousands of spares!

AWESOME JAWS

A shark's upper and lower jaws are stacked with rows of razor-sharp chompers— a lifetime supply!

CUTTING EDGE

Some sharks have pointy teeth for grabbing. Others have jagged triangular teeth for ripping.

No DENTISTS for me!

Great white shark

MOMENT OF TOOTH
If a tooth tumbles out, no problem! A new one shifts from the row behind to replace it.

LOST AND FOUND
Sharks lose and replace as many as 2,000 teeth each year!

Sharks even have teeth on their skin! Why? **To help them** swim faster.

Sharkskin with toothlike scales

Tasseled wobbegong shark

Sharks have senses that are more like superpowers.

SHARK SENSES

Imagine fumbling through the murky sea using just your eyesight. Sharks "see" their world in other amazing ways ...

SUPER SMELL
Some species of sharks can detect a drop of blood in an Olympic-size swimming pool!

I can
sense your
HEARTBEAT!

Whitetip reef sharks

SUPER TOUCH
Sensors along a shark's body read pressure changes in the water, such as from the flailing of a sick fish.

SUPER STRANGE
Shark heads are covered with tiny holes that detect the electrical signals given off by the muscles and brains of their prey.

23

Sharks use all these powers to hunt. And they'll eat almost anything.

Basking shark

Hammerhead shark

Salmon shark

FEEDING FRENZY!

Itty-bitty shrimps, blubbery sea lions, turtles, crabs, seabirds—if it lives in (or near) the ocean, it's on the menu! The biggest sharks—whale sharks and basking sharks—snack on tiny creatures called plankton. Great white sharks chase seals and sea lions. Hammerheads use their funny-shaped heads to hunt stingrays. Some sharks even chomp on other sharks! Sharks also scavenge dead and sick animals. Their anything-goes diet helps keep the oceans healthy and clean!

I'm on a **SEAFOOD** diet. I see food, I eat it.

Lemon shark

Sharks might seem scary, but most aren't dangerous to people.

You guys wanna HANG OUT sometime?

Caribbean reef shark

I'll stick with FISH, thank you.

Oceanic whitetip shark

Sharks hardly ever bite humans, and if they do it's usually by accident.

THREE SCARIEST SHARKS

Don't be afraid of the water—you have little to fear from sharks. People aren't on the menu. Scientists think shark attacks on humans, which are rare, are cases of mistaken identity. A shark sees a swimmer and confuses them for a tasty fish. When attacks do happen, one of these three fish is usually the culprit ...

GREAT WHITE SHARKS

The most feared fish in the ocean, the mighty great white can grow to more than 20 feet (6 m) long. These sharks are also famous for "breaching"—leaping out of the water as they ambush prey from below.

Great white shark

BULL SHARKS

These stocky sharks are famous for their mean attitudes. They can also swim in both salt and freshwater. Imagine jumping in a river and getting bumped by a bull shark. It's happened!

TIGER SHARKS

Sometimes called the garbage cans of the ocean, tiger sharks will munch on anything that crosses their snouts.

Bull shark

Tiger shark

Sharks are a very important part of our oceans. Since they're at the top of the food chain, they keep the balance of life in order. Humans must help protect sharks because ...

... we're kind of a BIG DEAL.

Lemon shark

Published by National Geographic Partners, LLC. All rights reserved.
Reproduction of the whole or any part of the contents without
written permission from the publisher is prohibited.

Since 1888, the National Geographic Society has funded more than
12,000 research, exploration, and preservation projects around
the world. The Society receives funds from National Geographic
Partners, LLC, funded in part by your purchase. A portion of the
proceeds from this book supports this vital work. To learn more,
visit natgeo.com/info.

NATIONAL GEOGRAPHIC and Yellow Border Design are trademarks
of the National Geographic Society, used under license.

For more information, visit nationalgeographic.com,
call 1-800-647-5463, or write to the following address:

National Geographic Partners
1145 17th Street N.W.
Washington, D.C. 20036-4688 U.S.A.

Visit us online at nationalgeographic.com/books

For librarians and teachers: ngchildrensbooks.org

More for kids from National Geographic: natgeokids.com

National Geographic Kids magazine inspires children to
explore their world with fun yet educational articles on animals,
science, nature, and more. Using fresh storytelling and amazing
photography, Nat Geo Kids shows kids ages 6 to 14 the fascinating
truth about the world—and why they should care.
kids.nationalgeographic.com/subscribe

For information about special discounts for bulk purchases,
please contact National Geographic Books Special Sales:
specialsales@natgeo.com

For rights or permissions inquiries, please contact National
Geographic Books Subsidiary Rights: bookrights@natgeo.com

Designed by Julide Dengel
Written by Crispin Boyer

The publisher would like to thank everyone who worked to
make this book come together: Rebecca Baines, editor; Shannon
Hibberd, photo editor; Alix Inchausti, production editor; and
Anne LeongSon and Gus Tello, design production assistants.

PHOTO CREDITS:
GI=Getty Images; MP=Minden Pictures; NGC=National Geographi
Creative; SS=Shutterstock
FRONT COVER: (UP RT), Rich Carey/SS; (LE, RT), Brian J. Skerry/
NGC; (CTR), Design Pics Inc/NGC; (CTR RT), Kletr/SS; (LO), LeonP/
SPINE, Brian J. Skerry/NGC; BACK COVER: (LE), Brian J. Skerry/NGC
(RT), frantisekhojdysz/SS; 1, Brian J. Skerry/NGC; 3, Uli Kunz/NGC;
5, wildestanimal/GI; 6, Ronald C. Modra/Sports Imagery/GI; 6-7,
Dennis Scott/GI; 7, wildestanimal/SS; 9, © David Fleetham/Nature
Picture Library; 10 (LE), Brian J. Skerry/NGC; 10 (RT), Paulo Oliveira/
Alamy; 11 (UP), Jones/Shimlock/Secret Sea Visions/GI; 11 (LO LE),
Carl Roessler/Digital Vision/NGC; 11 (LO RT), Kelvin Aitken/Alamy;
12, ribeiroantonio/SS; 13, Brian J. Skerry/NGC; 15, wildestanimal/
GI; 16-17, Mauricio Handler/NGC; 17 (UP LE), Norbert Wu/MP; 17 (U
RT), Kazuhiro Nogi/AFP/GI; 17 (CTR), Doug Perrine/MP; 17 (LO LE),
Mark Conlin/GI; 17 (LO RT), Solvin Zankl/MP; 18, Dave Fleetham/
GI; 19 (UP), Martin Prochazkacz/SS; 19 (LO LE), Matt9122/SS; 19 (LO
RT), MPcz/SS; 20, Photo Researchers Inc/NGC; 21, Jason Edwards/
NGC; 22, Global Pics/GI; 23 (UP), Jeff Rotman/MP; 23 (LO LE), Mique
Armengol/Barcroft Media/GI; 23 (LO RT), Tim Fitzharris/MP; 24, (LE
Alex Mustard/MP; 24 (CTR), Jeff Rotman/MP; 24 (RT), Doug Perrine
MP; 25, Fiona Ayerst/SS; 27, Jeff Rotman/GI; 28-29, Brian J. Skerry/
NGC; 29 (UP RT), wildestanimal/SS; 29 (LO LE), Education Images/
UIG via GI; 29 (LO RT), Mike Parry/MP; 30-31, Luiz Felipe V. Puntelr/
SS; 32, Kietr/SS

Hardcover ISBN:
978-1-4263-3361-3
Reinforced library binding
ISBN: 978-1-4263-3362-0

Printed in China
18/PPS/1

What's a
shark's favorite
sandwich?
Peanut butter
and jellyfish.

Hammerhead shark